Our God Reigns
Inspirational Prophetic Christian Poetry

Volume 2

Deborah Esther Nyamekye

© August 2016 Light of the World-John8.12 Publishing

All rights reserved.
ISBN: 978-0-9931738-7-5

DEDICATION

I dedicate this book to the Holy Spirit of God the Creator and Father who came to earth in the person of my Lord and Saviour Jesus Christ. Words cannot express the depth of my gratitude for the Holy Spirit's faithfulness in transforming my life and empowering me.

The Holy Spirit has also painstakingly taught me to partner wholeheartedly with God and in so doing I have over the years experienced deliverance and healing as well as fulfillment of prophetic destiny in a way I would never have imagined. An example is the mandate to write for the glory of God which in so doing birthed these volumes of poetry books among others.

Our God Reigns! Let the Earth Rejoice!

CONTENTS

Chapter 1   **INTIMACY WITH GOD & LIFE IN HIS SERVICE**   1

1. Find Rest in God at all Times
2. On the Joy Train I Go!
3. Abiding & Serving in God's House
4. Finding God in Silence
5. God's Bridge of Love
6. Intimacy with Purpose
7. The Calling
8. My Desire for His Things
9. I Surrender
10. Mission Accomplished
11. A Worshipful Life
12. God is in Control
13. Perfect Peace

Chapter 2   **REDEMPTION BY JESUS CHRIST, THE MESSIAH**   14

A. A BELIEVER'S TESTIMONY OF REDEMPTION & SURRENDER

1. The I Am & I
2. The Return
3. To Jesus, My Merciful Advocate
4. My Beloved & I
5. I Am Home
6. Come With Me
7. Altar of Sacrifice

B. REDEMPTION STORY TELLING (FICTITIOUS CHARACTERS)

8. The Great Escape
9. One Way Ticket to Heaven on the Metro
10. Jesus Heals the Brokenhearted & Sets the Captives Free
11. Restoration from Failures of Bygone Years

Chapter 3   **PROPHETIC ENCOURAGEMENT**   29
- God's Control of One's Identity, Purpose & Destiny
- God's Promises and Blessings

1. Waterfall of Blessings
2. Appointed Time of Recompense
3. Arise and Reclaim
4. God Brings Dreams to Pass
5. A Message unstoppable

Chapter 1

INTIMACY WITH GOD & LIFE IN HIS SERVICE

Find Rest in God at all Times

Find Rest, O my soul, in God alone, my hope comes from Him. He alone is my rock and my salvation; He is my fortress,
I will not be shaken.

Be calm, O my soul! I rest in the strength of God's arms and remember that no harm comes to those who put their trust in Him
at all times.

At all times, I am armed with His power,
How long will you frame lies for the assault? I will not be moved.
No longer do I bow before the seat of an idol,
for I am hidden in God's citadel.
"…my mighty rock, my refuge is God" [1]
at all times.

Scriptural inspiration: Psalm 62:5-6 Quote 1. Psalm 62:7 (ESV)

On the Joy Train I Go!

Introduction:
Oh the exuberant joy of being in the mission field! This focused missionary is expressing themselves gloriously as they travel the world ministering healing and preaching the Word of God. The glorious Heavenly Jerusalem, the abode of God Almighty is their joyful focus as they go forth.

        On the Joy Train I Go!
Rejoicing across the terrain and giving
"beauty for ashes and the oil of joy for mourning"[1]
     A-clapping and a-dancing I go
       doing the tango in Amarillo
        and tap dancing in Rio
     all to the praise of my King.

For its a new day, a new season
to cross the ocean with the risen Son,
now that's a reason to be a-clapping
       and a-dancing.
Not counting the days nor the cost,

I make some noise for he who found me
when I was lost.

Traversing the tunnel to Guadeloupe as
funnels of godly hope our choir sings
"the prospect of the righteous is joy, but
the hope of the wicked will perish"[2]

In every place off the train, I make the Gospel
plain saying "I have told you these things
so that you will be filled with"[3]
the joy of Christ my King.

A-clapping and a-dancing on the Joy Train I go
with sheep of a holy pedigree in tow
destined for the Heavenly Jerusalem we go!
"All you nations clap your hands! Shout out to God in
celebration![4]"

Scriptural inspiration: Quotes 1-4: 1.Isaiah 61:3 (KJV) 2.Proverbs 10:28(WEB) 3. John 15:11 (NTL) 4. Psalm 47:1 (NET)

Abiding & Serving in God's House

**

When I am out of your house O God,
I yearn for your abiding presence as fish cast
on dry ground long for water.
Abiding in you, I rest in your embrace
and find peace from the rat race.

To hear you say "well done good and
faithful servant " [1] is better than a mouthful
of praise from workers of iniquity.

Living a day in your house and in service
among your saints is worth more than a
thousand days elsewhere.

I would rather dwell in a mud hut with bare
necessities serving my God than in a mansion
full of frivolities serving nations' gods.

For God is my refuge
and shields me from
life's deluge.
He teaches my hands to
battle and by His Spirit,
I am set on fire,
empowered for His works
with no time to tire.

God's gifts are at my disposal
and His works, for my perusal.
God's light I am in the midst of
darkness that men would flee from
sin to yearn and seek the one thing:

That they may dwell in the house of the LORD all the days of their lives
"to behold the beauty of the LORD, and to inquire in His temple."[2]

Scriptural inspiration: Psalm 84:1-2, 10-12. Quotes: 1. Matthew 25:21, 23 2. Psalm 27:4

---------------- * ----------------

Finding God in Silence

**

Loving God,
teach me to be silent,
so that I can stay close to you
and listen as you speak
within my heart and through
what I see, hear and what men speak.

In silence, I listen and find you in me.

In every living thing, the life cycle
and life's ups and downs your
voice can be heard and your presence felt.

In silence, I listen and find you in everything.

I thank you for your gift of silence
as a cord linking me to your heart
and as a key that unlocks your
treasured words of truth into mine.

In silence, I listen and find you in me.

Inspired at a Quiet Day Retreat entitled
"Stay with Me" (practicing silence) on 23/03/2016

God's Bridge of Love

You are a bridge of love for your
neighbour to traverse and
progress in my love,
no more to transgress and
so drown in sin.

Your neighbor is anyone who
favours my unconditional love
or labours for artificial love.

Pour upon me your love and my
treasury shall release plenty
into your poverty.
You shall see my face
unveiled, for at my gaze
shall you know your worth.

When you walk with me as
my bride and talk of me with pride
as a living sacrifice and demonstrate
my love to the loveless,

promote my Word to enemies
and use the key of forgiveness,
then shall I draw near to you
and shall show you forth as a shofar
with the sound "GOD IS LOVE"[1],
and as a passage of refuge for multitudes
to know and abide in my LOVE.

Scriptural inspiration: Matthew 22:36-40. Quote: 1. 1 John 4:8

*

Intimacy with Purpose

Almighty God,
dwelling in thy Secret Place I see thy face
and I am love struck and stricken by thy grace.
I have nothing in my palms to give thee as a
holy offering of alms, so I give myself to thee
as a babe cradled in thy arms.

I abide under the shadow of the Almighty, not so that I can sleep,
oblivious to the trillions of issues in the deep,
but so that I can learn to discern thy will,
be strong in the power of thy might and
emit thy light as a city set on a hill.

"You are the light of the world like a city on a hilltop that cannot be hidden. No one lights a lamp and then puts it under a basket. Instead, a lamp is placed on a stand, where it gives light to everyone in the house. In the same way, let your good deeds shine out for all to see, so that everyone will praise your heavenly Father". (Matthew 5:14-16 NLT)

Scriptural inspiration: Psalm 91:1, Eph.6:10

The Calling

A state of mind in
tandem with emotions
rejoicing on a bright day.

A merry heart
doth emit a smile
as a beaming ray.

A light set on a hill
illuminating a dark
world, healing hearts
day by day.

Scriptural inspiration: Matthew 5:14-16

———— * ————

My Desire for His Things
**

To have all things
The Kingdom I first seek.
To do all things
Christ's strength I entreat.

One thing I desire
is what I do seek:
To abide in God,

His beauty to behold
and enquire in His abode.
To savour His Word
and rest in His favour.

One main thing I desire is
what I do seek:
To heal the sick and
strengthen the weak,
and to feed the hungry the Word of Truth
for the ways of the Father to take solid root.

Scriptural inspiration: The Gospels, John14:12, Matt. 6:33/Phil 4:13, Psalm 27:4

I Surrender
**

I pray, how can I die to sinful Self,
and do the good I want to do,
to abide in God's presence
and in His will?

Where will pride take me?
Out of His presence, out of His will.
*"God resists the proud, but gives grace
to the humble"*
I surrender to
Almighty God,
Everlasting Father.

Where will carnality take me?
Out of His presence, out of His will.
*"For to be carnally minded is death; but to be
spiritually minded is life and peace."*

I surrender to
Life-giving Spirit,
Prince of Peace.
By Him, I am justified and
sanctified in His likeness.

*"For as many as are led by the Spirit of God,
they are the sons of God"*.
I surrender to
Holy Spirit,
River of Life.
By Him, I am led to
Father's Heart.
Free to know His mind
and discern His ways.

I surrender to
Father
Son and
Holy Ghost.
Abiding in His presence, praying
"Thy Kingdom come, Thy will be done on Earth, as *it is* in heaven."[1]

Scriptural inspiration: Romans 7, Romans 8:6, 14, 1 Peter 5:5, 1 Corinth. 2, Psalm 16:11
Quote 1: Matt 6:10 KJV

Mission Accomplished
**

An army is raised.
On a mission of revival,
with chivalry to shut
doors of division and rivalry.
Realms of unity are open
and strength imparted.
Blessed, with joy

they choose to serve.

The stray as prodigals
welcomed and
cleansed from guile.
Justice rendered,
freedom from trials.
Impacted, with joy
they choose to stay.

Scriptural inspiration: Matthew 28:19-20, Isaiah 25:4, John 17:21, Isaiah 58:6-12.

———— * ————

A Worshipful Life
**

I will lift my hands in praise.
I will bow my knees in worship.
I will lay me down in surrender to
my Maker,
my Master,
my King.

I will proclaim the Word.
I will speak the truth.
I will tell my story of
His adoration,
His salvation,
His restoration.

I will give to the poor.
I will help the weak.
I will pray for the sick,
in obedience to

His call,
His command,
His petition,
"for we are his workmanship, created in Christ Jesus unto good works, which God hath before ordained that we should walk in them." (Eph.2:10KJV)

---- * ----

God is in Control
**

When the world offends me
God defends me for
He has my back.

When the world disowns me
I remember God owns me
and promises I will never lack.

When the world disappointed me
God appoints me in His
abode and keeps me on track.

Lacking nothing, nor back-tracking,
in victory, I march on declaring
"God is in Control"

Perfect Peace
**

Thou wilt keep him in perfect peace, whose mind is stayed on thee: because he trusteth in thee. (Isaiah 26:3 KJV)

Perfect peace is Father's reward He entreats
to mindsets stayed on Him in intimate retreat.

Perfect peace is Father's mealtime treat
so we can calmly say
"…my meat is to do the will of him
that sent me"[1]

Perfect Peace is Father's empowering gift
so we can boldly say
"I am not miffed, I labour under
divine favour!"

At Father's Banquet Table,
rewarded, we feast on meat in fervour
and drink the zeal of divine favour.

On the Mission Field,
commissioned, our works
"Speak and preach Perfect Peace
to change mindsets and speech"[2].

Chapter 2

REDEMPTION BY JESUS CHRIST, THE MESSIAH

-A BELIEVER'S TESTIMONY OF REDEMPTION & SURRENDER

-REDEMPTION STORY TELLING (FICTITIOUS CHARACTERS)

A BELIEVER'S TESTIMONY OF REDEMPTION

The I Am & I

The I Am made me who I am.
He created me and from my mother's womb
gave me free will to choose life or the tomb.
I chose the tomb.

The I Am made me who I am.
He created me anew, for in Christ I was redeemed.
Snatched from the serpent's womb,
no more in the tomb,
I am washed in the blood
recreated in "Christ Jesus unto good works."[1]
I choose life.

Scriptural inspiration: New Testament. Quote 1: Ephesians 2:10.

*
___ ___

The Return

I longed to return to the Garden
where man walked with His Maker
in the cool of day
so he found his way.

I longed to return to the Bosom
of Abba Father
cradled far away from the prey,
no more to stray.

He heard me and with His rod and staff
led me into His Garden paths of righteousness.

So I returned from perilous places I tread,
singing "Hallelujah, I am free from captors I dread!"

My return is as sweet as "milk and honey" in a land of plenty.
In this place, the shelter of the Most High God,

I dwell forever and gaze
upon His beauty.

I am protected and exalted
above my enemies.

I am blessed and highly
favoured.

"…I will offer in his tent sacrifices with shouts of joy;
I will sing and make melody to the LORD"[1]

Scriptural inspiration: Genesis 1-2, Exodus 33:3, Psalms 23,
27:4-6, 91. Quote 1: Psalm 27:6 ESV

To Jesus, My Merciful Advocate
**

In the sound of each lash
endured for my sake I hear
"Go, you are made whole"

At the sight of your bruised flesh
I see upon you my offence to
relieve me from self-defense.

In the pouring of your blood my
righteousness as filthy rags is
washed clean.

In your death was my death.
At your resurrection I arose.
In your Law that governs my new life
is my acquittal from the Law of sin and death.

Thank you, Jesus, Most Merciful Advocate.

"...if anyone does sin, we have an advocate who pleads our case before the Father. He is Jesus Christ, the one who is truly righteous. He himself is the sacrifice that atones for our sins—and not only our sins but the sins of all the world." (1 John 2:1-2 NLT).

Scriptural inspiration: The New Testament - Romans 8:1-3, Isaiah 53

My Beloved & I
**

I am my Beloved's, and my Beloved is mine.
His only begotten Son He sent to prove His love for me.
A Son so compassionate, he took my place on a tree,
With nail pierced palms and blood drenched scars,
He gave up the ghost.

I was with him in betrayal, mockery, and shame.
One with him in the grave released by his power
and free to escape on his train.

I am with him in liberty.
One with him in glory,
with the keys of heaven and earth,
forever to conquer and reign.

Free from shackles of sin,
with a signet ring betrothed to my redeemer groom,
forever to sing:

"I am my Beloved's, and my Beloved is mine"[1]

Scriptural inspiration: The Gospels, Isaiah 53.
Quote 1: Song of Songs 6:3

I Am Home
**

By your breath you gave me life,
with precision you formed me,
I crawled, I walk, I run.

By a new release of your breath you restored me.
With perfection you re-formed me,
I hope, I advance and I'm unstoppable.

In you I live and move and have my being.
You say "call on me", "come up higher".
With humble adoration and dance
I call and come to you.

"I am home. Renew me day by day."

Scriptural inspiration: Genesis 1:27, Acts 17:28, Revelations 4:1,
Jeremiah 33:3, Psalm 51

Come With Me

Searching?
Come with me!

I am heading somewhere.
Where there is no night only day,
Where there is no sadness only joy,
With a mansion made ready for me.
A place where with angels
I'll be praising and dancing all day.

Come with me to the heavenly place,
no need for accolades, tickets or proof of a trade.
All you need is to follow the Good Shepherd,
the Rock and Steady WAY.

Are you ready?
Come with me!

———— * ————

Altar of Sacrifice
**

At the Altar of Sacrifice
I arise from the fall,
surrendering before God,
I give Him my all.

My all is giving of my heart
and that is where I start.

My all is offering what's so dear
'cause of reverential fear.

At the Altar of Sacrifice,
I give my all
to stand tall before the LORD.

My all is loving mankind
as I am loved by God
who is one of a kind.

My all is giving up my life for
friends and praying for my foes.

Always ready to pay a price,
I surrender all
at the Altar of Sacrifice.

REDEMPTION STORY TELLING (FICTITIOUS CHARACTERS)

The Great Escape

**

A Great Tribulation is upon the people;
I hear the sound of their hurried strides and
thundering groans as they descend from
their elevated thrones.

The people are in agony and unbearable pain,
with bodies jerking as struck by lightning and

tears dropping from darkened eyes as ice
pellets crushing down from the skies.

A Great Awakening is upon the people;
They see the source of their worldly ways is
the cause of ripples leading to floods of suffering and
of seeds growing into trees of hateful deeds.

The people are repentant with unsearchable gain.
Many a path have they trodden that leads to death,
but now they have found a Way of Escape in their new birth.

Their futile lives, they now offer to Jesus Christ
in exchange for Jubilees of peace, sumptuous treats
and righteous deeds, so they joyfully sing:

"Praise the Lord; praise God our Saviour! For each day he carries us in His arms. Our God is a God who saves! The Sovereign LORD rescues us from death.[1]"

Scriptural Quote 1. Psalm 68:19-20 (NLT).

Note: We give glory and praise to God who arises and scatters His enemies (Ps. 68:1) and redeems us from spiritual death imparting His righteousness, peace and joy through our Lord and Saviour Jesus Christ.

One Way Ticket to Heaven on the Metro

**

Riding on the London Metro
late one evening turning to the left,
I saw a man standing, swaying back and forth.
He ruffled his hair and shouted
"This goes to Euston Square,
how do we get a train to Euston!"
"Get a new brain Dr. Triston!"
a woman jeered.
"A rage filled man approached the
noisy pair, shook his fists and said
"one more word from you two and
I'll leave you as good as dead!"

Turning my gaze away, I imagined
Dr. Triston's life what was, is and is to
come. I pictured him in his surgery,
bespectacled with nicely groomed hair,
busy and respectable seated in his chair.
He began the day in his surgery sober,
then off he went to the social bar
and then picked up this tart!

Rolling my eyes, I began to imagine
this woman's seedy life
but suddenly I heard the doctor say
"a penny for your thoughts, me lady".
I shook my head nervously as sly as a fox.
"Do you know Christ, who is God's Son...?"

"Euston is on the Northern line"
I said cutting him short.
"God's calling you on this main line
through Jesus Christ His Son".
I sighed and thought "He's had too much to
drink and sounds so thick!"
Then I asked "Dr. Triston, who is this Son?!"

"My name is Marlon Jones, my wife
is Martha and we live for God.
Acting is my vocation;
tonight I played the part of Dr. Triston,
who became a friend of Christ Jesus,
the great physician.

Marlon testified of his miraculous
healing and his journey from
the occult to Christ.
He left a life of vice, went back twice
but finally the prodigal
learnt what was right, and
now speaks of Christ with love and
obeys his commands from above.

He said "I present my Saviour
to you this day,
but know, this is not a play
and I have much to say,
'cause of time, I can't but
tell a thing or two and
hope that you would want to know him too."

Marlon spoke a great deal and oh I felt such a fool,
for I imagined he was a drunk and
to be frank, I thought his Mrs. was one too!
I listened to his blessed words.
His voice was as the sound of one drunk, not with wine,
but God's Spirit and his eyes were diluted with tears of love.

"Could I a sinner, whose mouth is full of venom,
eyes aglow with hatred and a mind clogged with filth,
ever be like Marlon and his wife?

As one who read my mind, Martha
began to say "There is no condemnation
for those in Christ, for what He did for us,
God can do for you!"
I felt the power I knew was God,
like a mower it started to work,
for I began to holler "Lord Jesus,
I need you in my life! Come teach me
to be holy and make me whole!!"

Martha and Marlon hugged me and
from deep within these words I heard:
"My precious child welcome to where your belong,
for before your birth in Montreal,
this day was planned, that you will
have your one way ticket to heaven on the Metro".

Jesus said of himself "For the Son of Man
came to seek and save those who are lost."[1]

Scriptural inspiration: The New Testament /Gospels Quote 1: Luke 19:10 NLT

"1Therefore there is now no condemnation for those who are in Christ Jesus. 2For the law of the Spirit of life in Christ Jesus has set you free from the law of sin and of death. 3For what the Law could not do, weak as it was through the flesh, God did: sending His own Son in the likeness of sinful flesh and as an offering for sin, He condemned sin in the flesh" (Romans 8:1-3).

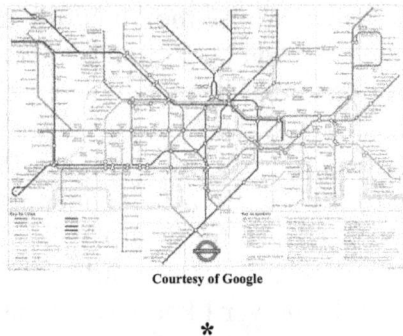
Courtesy of Google

*

Jesus Heals the Broken Hearted & Sets the Captives Free

It was the bleak mid-winter, and it felt the same within his heart,
as day after day the memories flooded his mind with such force
that he was drowning in despair and wept until his voice was
hoarse.

The young man was feeling crushed
'cause once again his efforts were trashed.
Every time he thought he was in the money,
it was like there was a hole in his bag of cash.

In his love life things were the same
for his advances made no difference as many
a woman would shrug and walk away, as if
to say "you're not my type, you're a mug!'

He remembered the days when he sought fame
and had friends in high places with whom he
bet at the races. He tried to be like them but his photo shoots
were returned with the message "sorry mate,
modeling is not your fate!" So he auditioned to sing and
also thought acting was his thing, but his agent came back to say
"they say try something else 'cause acting and singing
are not your thing!"

He was classed among world losers,
subject to many teasers, state allowances and
family loan advances. Rejected and dejected,
he cried "no one would care less if I self-ejected!"

There was a knock on the door and in came his
brother-in-law, handing him a Bible he said
"heard your voice message, let's hear God's voice in
this life-giving message."

That was me ten years ago, I am no longer under the Law,
but saved by Grace thanks to my brother-in-law,
no longer fired up with envy, but ignited with God's power
and street savvy for the redeemer.

I married a woman, sent by God who says
"blessed be the Lord, He sent a man who's my type!"
We hand out bibles for the harvest is ripe and
preach the Gospel every season to deliver
men from strife and treason against Christ the King.

For this reason, hear me one and all,
Christ will do for you what he did for me,
promised when he said:

"The Spirit of the Sovereign LORD is upon me, for the LORD
has anointed me to bring good news to the poor. He has sent me to
comfort the brokenhearted and to proclaim that captives will be
released and prisoners will be freed[1]"

Scriptural inspiration: The New Testament. Quote 1. Isaiah 61:1 (NLT)

Restoration from Failures of Bygone Years

Introduction
This is a story of a Christian addicted to spending, living as though there is no tomorrow, and then finding themselves destitute. This is what happens when we make financial decisions without applying God given wisdom and common sense. All is not lost; we have a God who is merciful and is in the business of restoring our lives. Let us seek him daily in prayer for His wisdom and direction in every area of our lives.

Once upon a time,
You lived in a trance and money was spent even at a glance.
You emptied the till to buy at a whim.
When the bills came with a senseless grin you exclaimed
"Oh never mind, you only live once, enjoy it while it lasts"

Today there is the stench of a decaying business,
and the sight of a home barred for repossession.
A reminder of money wasted as sewage down the drain.

Now there is no hope for tomorrow, and times are hard
so that you chew your meat down to the bone marrow,
saying "money is tight I need to eat every bite!"

You utter not a word,
but your troubled face is as a pain-filled voice that says
"I am doomed" and you come out only at night with
a malnourished frame that's a haunting sight.

Dear beloved of God, do not let your heart be troubled,
nor hide in shame for we all have weaknesses
but God loves us all the same.
God beckons:
"Is anyone thirsty? Come and drink—even if
you have no money! Come, take your choice of

wine or milk it's all free!
[2] Why spend your money on food that does not give you strength? Why pay for food that does you no good? Listen to me, and you will eat what is good. You will enjoy the finest food.[1]"

Cast away your cup of dregs and receive
Christ's Covenant Cup, filled to the brim to
quench your thirst.

Trust God in your time of lack and He will do the rest.
He shall revive your life, repair personal and
business ruins and the menace to your finance,
He shall beat to dust.

"Trust in the LORD with all your heart;
do not depend on your own understanding.
Seek his will in all you do, and he will show you
which path to take[2]"

Quotes: 1. Isaiah 55:1-2 (NLT) 2. Prov.3:5-6 (NLT)

Chapter 3 PROPHETIC ENCOURAGEMENT

-God's Control of One's Identity, Purpose & Destiny
-God's Promises and Blessings

Waterfall of Blessings
**

INTRODUCTION:

This prophetic poem was borne out of what happened on the morning of 25th May 2016. I had a vision of a waterfall, and I had this sense that it represented a gushing down of blessings from God the Father. About two hours later a sister in Christ sent me a picture of a waterfall by text and at the end of the day, I felt inspired to write this poem.

The poem is a prophetic word that is not for me alone; this is a season when the floodgates of heaven are open for a mighty outpouring of what multitudes have been seeking from the LORD. I encourage you to partner with God in obedience and faithfulness for His will or promises to be fulfilled in your life.

I declare and decree God's abundant blessings upon you in Jesus' mighty name. Nothing is impossible for him or her who believes for God shall bring His will to pass in their lives. God is never too late but is always on time. May God fulfill your heart's desire according to His will in Jesus' mighty name Amen.

Cascading down is a mighty
waterfall, an avalanche of
blessings whose time has come.

A ripple effect is forming
crushing into binding fortes of
deception, chaos and
depression, it shows no
mercy breaking prison walls
and foundations.

It's power is for the
rebuilding of ruins,
restoration of destinies
and releasing of
righteousness, peace
and joy in its advancing.

It's your time of visitation for
a blessed outpouring.

Appointed Time of Recompense

**

Introduction:
This is a prophetic word of encouragement to those who have given up on the ungodly world to live for God through Christ. However, they are experiencing persecution and lack. Rest assured, we serve a God who not only hears and sees, but He also takes note and in His appointed time, recompenses and blesses those who are His and wait on Him.

Father knows you ended
the evil worldly game to
carry your cross in shame
to live your life for His fame.

He sees how you
refrain from giving up
under the strain of
a life of struggles and pain
and how you choose to sing
"By my God I am
always joyful,
full of gratitude,
Oh forever thankful".

He hears your
shouts of joy,
sonnets of gratitude,
and songs of thanksgiving.

Your voice of praise rises to the
skies until saturated heavenly
clouds can no more hold your
treasures reserved in storehouse
preserves.

Then there is a breaking
forth of abundant blessings,
mighty outpourings with
no end in sight.

Hurricanes of blessings,
Storms of rewards.
Receive!

The time of restoration
and recompense is now.
Receive!

"Do not hold back
for the time is now,
raise your hands"
says The LORD.
Receive!

———————*———————

Arise and Reclaim
**

It's time to arise and
reclaim your identity,
visions, dreams and destiny
for the enemy comes
again and again,
repeating old
deceptive tunes
as a broken record
and as a masked
dance partner waltzing
with you in "la la" land.

The Father of lies
creates an illusion
of truth, mocks you
day and night and
rocks your boat of life
with such tormenting
force stealing your
blessed goods until
you are provoked
to anchor at his docks,
and live in his
Hammock of death.

Not until you arise from
your slumber and sleep

will you know it is all a
charade to give you
an identity, a destiny that
sustains delusion and
restores your past of
abuse, rejection
and shame.

It's time to arise,
to proclaim your purpose.
It's time to reclaim
by faith what's yours.
"Take back your
possessions" says
Father of truth.

Arise and Reclaim.

SCRIPTURAL INSPIRATION (KJV):

John 10:10
10The thief cometh not, but for to steal, and to kill, and to destroy: I am come that they might have life, and that they might have [it] more abundantly. 11I am the good shepherd: the good shepherd giveth his life for the sheep.

Is. 52:1-3
1Awake, awake; put on thy strength, O Zion; put on thy beautiful garments, O Jerusalem, the holy city: for henceforth there shall no more come into thee the uncircumcised and the unclean.
2Shake thyself from the dust; arise, [and] sit down, O Jerusalem: loose thyself from the bands of thy neck, O captive daughter of Zion. 3For thus

saith the LORD, Ye have sold yourselves for nought; and ye shall be redeemed without money.

Is.60:1-5

1Arise, shine; for thy light is come, and the glory of the LORD is risen upon thee.
2For, behold, the darkness shall cover the earth, and gross darkness the people: but the LORD shall arise upon thee, and his glory shall be seen upon thee. 3And the Gentiles shall come to thy light, and kings to the brightness of thy rising. 4Lift up thine eyes round about, and see: all they gather themselves together, they come to thee: thy sons shall come from far, and thy daughters shall be nursed at [thy] side. 5Then thou shalt see, and flow together, and thine heart shall fear, and be enlarged; because the abundance of the sea shall be converted unto thee, the forces of the Gentiles shall come unto thee.

PRAYER:

Merciful Father, I pray for a great outpouring of your Spirit of wisdom, knowledge and understanding into the life of your children. LORD, I ask that you expose every deceiving spirit to us and give us the power to overcome.
With the authority invested in me through Christ Jesus I rebuke Satan, his demons and decree every work of Satan nullified by the blood of the Lamb.
I ask LORD that you would impart a great measure of the Spirit of discernment into the lives of your people and that we would increase in the knowledge of you and live victoriously in the identity and destiny you planned for us. In Jesus' mighty name I pray, Amen.

---*---

God Brings Dreams to Pass

Up and down the land she walked,
as a wanderer seeing naught and
feeling lost, she sighed and cried
"I have stalled 'cause of the fog and drought".

Even within, she felt barren and dry
wanting to pray but too weak to try.

Then came a light so bright before her face,
but looking around she saw no one in that place.
Within her heart, she heard a voice say loud & clear
"I am the Light of the World who loves you, my dear".

Then he placed a fountain in her heart and said
"Out of you shall flow rivers of living water
to quench your thirst, so you shall never falter".
Then suddenly her heart became a well-watered
verdant land, from her mouth was a melodious waterfall,
and her eyes were awash with God's salve.

The bright ray of the morning sun
hit her face so hard she covered her eyes and
exclaimed "my, what a dream so real!"
The dream spoke of God's Light,
His love and the River of Life, a picture of what
is to come, a revelation of God's delivering might
and abundant promises day and night.

Now strengthened, newly enlightened,
no more doubtful, newly hopeful,
she knew that she could cope
with every trial whatever the scope,
for her heart was now full of hope,
because of Him who said "I have spoken it,
I will also bring it to pass; I have purposed it,
I will also do it."[1]

Scriptural inspirations: John 8:12, 7:38-39. Quote 1: Isaiah 46:11 (KJV)

A message unstoppable

A message pushes
through a maze
unfazed by storms
and resisting
waves of life

It is unrelenting,
swerving around
obstacles,
arriving on time,
and on point.
Unstoppable as a
babe's delivery time.

It must be heard in this
generation
without alteration
nor additives
by those with motives
for an alternative.

It resonates tireless
across borders,
boundaries of land

and heart.
Turned on at full blast
A message to impart
and to trust

Day and night,
it is heard,
in all seasons
and for divine
reasons to heal
nations and relations.

Rain or shine
it resounds.
A powerful sound
as a two-edged sword
to cut away rigid trains of
thought.

It speaks "Humankind is precious, every life matters whatever the race. Consider, care, and love one another.
Love is the principal thing."

Note: I started writing this poem on the night of 19th July 2016 and honestly, I did not know in my natural mind what the "message" was, I fell asleep towards the end of it and when I woke up the next day, in the early hours, I got the "message" at the end of the poem as I have written it.

DT

³³ "This is the covenant I will make with the people of Israel
after that time," declares the LORD.
"I will put my law in their minds
and write it on their hearts.
I will be their God,
and they will be my people. (Jer.31:33 NLT)

²⁸ There is neither Jew nor Greek, there is neither bond nor free, there is
neither male nor female:
for ye are all one in Christ Jesus.
²⁹ And if ye be Christ's, then are ye Abraham's seed, and heirs according
to the promise.
(Gal 3:28-29 KJV)

For more information:
Bearwitness-Forerunner Ministries International
bearwitnessforerunner88@gmail.com

© August 2016 Light of the World-John8.12 Publishing

All rights reserved.
ISBN: 978-0-9931738-7-5

www.ingramcontent.com/pod-product-compliance
Lightning Source LLC
Chambersburg PA
CBHW061310040426
42444CB00010B/2576